I0439821

 Director of
Central
Intelligence

Director of Central Intelligence Directive No. 6/4

Personnel Security Standards and Procedures Governing Eligibility for Access to Sensitive Compartemented Information

02 July 1998

DIRECTOR OF CENTRAL INTELLIGENCE DIRECTIVE

6/4

PERSONNEL SECURITY STANDARDS AND PROCEDURES GOVERNING ELIGIBILITY FOR ACCESS TO SENSITIVE COMPARTMENTED INFORMATION (SCI)

This directive supersedes Director of Central Intelligence Directive 1/14, as amended 12 August 1994.

(Effective Date: 02 July 1998)

A complete copy of DCID 6/4 now consists of the basic DCID and Annexes A through F, as follows:

- Annex A - Investigative Standards for Background Investigations for Access to Classified Information.

- Annex B - Quality Control Guidelines for the Single Scope Background Investigation.

- Annex C - Adjudication Guidelines for Determining Eligibility for Access to Classified Information.

- Annex D - Appeals Procedures: Denial or Revocation of Access.

- Annex E - Standards for SCI Security Awareness Programs in the US Intelligence Community.

- Annex F - Reciprocity of SCI Eligibility Determinations (Annex F was created subsequent to the creation of the DCID. The DCI approved Annex F on 13 Oct 99.)

The President approved the Adjudicative Guidelines, Temporary Eligibility Standards and Investigative Standards required by Executive Order 12968 on March 24, 1997. This revised DCID incorporates the President's policy documents verbatim, at Annexes A and C, to promote the use of these common and consistent standards for government-wide security background investigations.

These two annexes should be read in the context of the Director of Central Intelligence (DCI) special authorities, governing access eligibility to SCI, although the actual wording addresses a broader application to clearance actions.

The DCI exercises authority derived from statute and executive order over access eligibility to SCI and delegates this authority to Determination Authorities through Senior Officials of the Intelligence Community. (See Definitions.) Nothing in this directive or its annexes shall be deemed to preclude the DCI or the DDCI under the authority of the National Security Act of 1947, as amended, from taking any actions regarding an individual's SCI access.

Pursuant to the provisions of the National Security Act of 1947, as amended, and Executive Orders 12333 and 12968, the following personnel security guidelines, procedures, standards, and continuing security programs are hereby established for all US Government civilian and military personnel, consultants, contractors, employees of contractors, and other individuals who require access to SCI. Individual departments and agencies may establish such additional security steps as may be deemed necessary and appropriate to resolve issues and/or address employment standards unique to them to ensure that effective security is maintained.

1. Definitions.

a. Cohabitant--A person living in a spouse-like relationship with the individual requiring SCI information.

b. Compelling Need--A signed determination by a Senior Official of the Intelligence Community (SOIC) or his/her designee that the services of an individual are deemed essential to operation or mission accomplishment.

c. Risk Assessment--A written evaluation supporting the adjudicative process, especially when a significant exception to a Personnel Security Standard is being considered. This assessment should consist of an evaluation from security, counterintelligence, and other technical or management experts as appropriate, and should contrast the compelling national security benefit of an individual accessed to SCI with the risk.

d. Determination Authority--A designee of a SOIC with responsibility for decisions rendered with respect to SCI access eligibility or ineligibility.

e. Immediate Family--The spouse, parents, siblings, children, and cohabitant of the individual requiring SCI access.

f. Intelligence Community--Those US Government organizations and activities identified in the National Security Act of 1947, as amended, 50 USC 401a(4), EO 12333, or successor orders, as making up such a Community.

g. Senior Officials of the Intelligence Community (SOICs)--The heads of organizations or activities within the Intelligence Community, as defined by the National Security Act of 1947, as amended, 50 USC 401a(4), and EO 12333.

h. Sensitive Compartmented Information--Classified information concerning or derived from intelligence sources, methods, or analytical processes requiring handling exclusively within formal access control systems established by the DCI.

2. Purpose.

The purpose of this directive is to enhance the security protection of SCI through the application of personnel security standards, procedures, and continuing security programs.

3. Applicability.

The provisions of this directive will apply to all persons (other than elected officials of the US Government, to include elected State Governors as may be required on an individual basis, Federal judges, and those individuals for whom the DCI makes a specific exception) without regard to a civilian or military status, form of employment, official rank or position, or length of service. This directive does not apply to situations involving the duly authorized disclosure of SCI to representatives of foreign governments and international organizations.

4. General.

a. The granting of access to SCI will be controlled under the strictest application of the "need-to-know" principle and in accordance with the personnel security standards and procedures set forth in this directive.

b. In accordance with DCID 1/19, "Security Policy for Sensitive Compartmented Information," and its supplement, "DCID 1/19 Security Policy Manual," those approved for access to SCI are required to sign a DCI-authorized nondisclosure agreement that includes a provision for prepublication review as a condition of access to SCI.

5. Personnel Security Standards.

Criteria for security approval of an individual on a need-to-know basis for access to SCI are as follows:

a. The individual requiring access to SCI must be a US citizen.

b. The individual's immediate family must also be US citizens.

c. Members of the individual's immediate family and any other persons to whom he or she is bound by affection or obligation should neither be subject to physical, mental, or other forms of duress by a foreign power or by persons who may be or have been engaged in criminal activity, nor advocate the use of force or violence to overthrow the Government of the United States or the alteration of the form of Government of the United States by unconstitutional means.

d. The individual must be stable; trustworthy; reliable; of excellent character, judgment, and discretion; and of unquestioned loyalty to the United States.

6. Exceptions to Personnel Security Standards.

Any exception to the Personnel Security Standards will be a common sense determination based on the fact that the available information supports a finding that the specific risk to national security is manageable in the specific case for which the exception is granted. The organization determining that an exception is warranted will document their finding in the individual's security record. As appropriate, a risk assessment, normally directed by the Determination Authority, may be required to aid in the determination of the appropriateness of granting an exception to one of the Personnel Security Standards. If accomplished, this assessment should become a part of the individual's security record.

a. The DCI is the exclusive authority for granting an exception to the requirement that the Subject be a US citizen.

b. The affected SOIC or specified designee may grant exception to the standard requiring US citizenship for the family members of an individual proposed for SCI access, as well as the standard requiring individuals to which Subject is bound by affection or obligation be free of any form of duress.

c. Exceptions to the US citizenship requirement for individuals to be accessed to SCI and their immediate family members shall require certification of a compelling need. This exception should be based upon a specific national security requirement and a certification of compelling need.

7. Investigative Requirements and Standards.

a. The investigation conducted on an individual under consideration for access to SCI will conform to the requirements of a Single Scope Background Investigation (SSBI) as defined in Annex A, "Investigative Standards for Background Investigations for Access to Classified Information." Quality Control procedures relevant to investigations are defined in Annex B, "Quality Control Guidelines for the Single Scope Background Investigation."

b. When conditions indicate, investigation of immediate family members will be conducted to the extent necessary to permit a determination by the adjudicating agency that the provisions of paragraph 5 of this directive are met.

c. Where a previous investigation has been conducted within the past five years that meets the standards of Annex A, it will serve as a basis for granting access approval except where there is substantial information indicating that the employee may not satisfy the adjudicative guidelines in Annex C. If a previous investigation does not meet the Annex A standards, if it is more than five years old, or if there is a break in SCI access of two years or more, a current investigation will be required but may be limited to that necessary to bring the individual's file up-to-date in accordance with the investigative requirements set forth in Annex A of this directive, paragraphs 6 and 10. The up-dating process may be limited to review of applicable records, starting with an updated SF-86, and involve reinvestigation only when it appears the person may no longer satisfy standards for access under this directive. Should new information be developed during the current investigation that bears unfavorably on the individual's activities covered by the previous investigation, the current inquiries will be expanded as necessary to develop full details of this information.

d. Programs will be instituted requiring the periodic reinvestigation (PR) of personnel provided access to SCI. These SSBI-PRs will be conducted in accordance with the procedures and scope contained in the section of Annex A defining the SSBI-PR. The SSBI-PR may be expanded as necessary to resolve outstanding issues.

e. Notwithstanding the status of an individual's background investigation, departments and agencies with policies sanctioning the use of the polygraph for personnel security purposes may require polygraph examinations when deemed necessary by the department or agency head to be in the national security interest of the United States. Where they exist, such polygraph programs shall be characterized by unified training and certification as well as by coordination of scope, applicability and fairness issues to promote consistency, reciprocity and due process.

f. In those cases in which the individual has lived outside of the United States for a substantial period, a thorough assessment of the adequacy of the investigation in terms of fulfillment of the investigative requirements and judicious review of the information therein must be made before an exception is considered.

8. Temporary Eligibility for Access to SCI.

a. In exceptional cases, including national emergency situations and hostilities involving US personnel, the SOIC or his designee may determine that it is necessary or advisable in the national interest to authorize temporary access to SCI before completion of the SSBI. In this situation, the procedures contained in the Annex A section entitled "Investigative Standards for Temporary Eligibility for Access" will be complied with before temporary access is permitted. A personal interview of the individual by trained security, investigative, or counterintelligence personnel will be conducted wherever possible and practicable.

b. The SSBI and final evaluation will be completed at the earliest practicable moment unless an exception is granted by the DCI. Temporary eligibility for access is valid only at the agency granting it and other agencies which expressly agree to accept it and acknowledge understanding of its investigative basis. Therefore, certification to other organizations of individuals authorized temporary access will include explicit notification of the fact.

c. Temporary eligibility for access may be granted only to SCI necessary for the individual to perform authorized functions. Therefore, indoctrination briefings will be modified to the basic information necessary to ensure protection of the SCI to which the individual will be exposed, and appropriate nondisclosure agreements signed.

9. Reporting Requirements.

Individuals who hold SCI access have special responsibilities and obligations to report to their cognizant security officer, in writing and when feasible in advance, activities, conduct or employment that could conflict with their ability to protect classified information from unauthorized disclosure or counterintelligence threats. A more detailed explanation and a listing of an individual's responsibilities and reporting requirements are contained in Annex E. In addition, initial and updated security documents (e.g. Statement of Personal History, Questionnaire for National Security Positions, Security Clearance Application) and security records shall include details of such employment, activities, associations and/or conduct to facilitate appropriate investigation and evaluation to determine whether the circumstances create an unacceptable risk to the security of SCI or of unauthorized disclosure. Annex C, Guideline L,

"Outside Activities," summarizes the concern.

10. Determinations of Access Eligibility.

The evaluation of the information developed by investigation of an individual's loyalty and suitability will be accomplished by trained professional adjudicators under the cognizance of the SOIC concerned. When all other information developed on an individual is favorable, a minor investigative requirement that has not been met should not preclude a favorable access determination by an authorized adjudicative authority. In all evaluations, the protection of the national security is paramount. Any doubt concerning personnel having access to SCI should be resolved in favor of the national security, and the access should be denied or revoked. The ultimate determination of whether the granting of access is clearly consistent with the interest of national security will be an overall common sense determination based on all available information. The adjudicative guidelines for determining eligibility for access to SCI are contained in Annex C.

11. Appeals Procedures.

Annex D prescribes common appeals procedures to be followed when an individual's SCI access has been denied or revoked.

12. Continuing Security Programs.

a. To facilitate attainment of appropriate standards of personnel security and to augment both the access approval criteria and the investigative requirements established by this directive, member departments and agencies shall institute continuing security programs based on risk management principles for all individuals having access to SCI. In addition to security indoctrinations (see Annex E, "Standards for SCI Security Awareness Programs in the US Intelligence Community"), these programs will be tailored to create mutually supporting procedures to identify and resolve issues which bring into question an individual's loyalty and integrity or suggest the possibility of his or her being subject to undue influence or duress through foreign relationships or exploitable personal conduct. These programs should include the capacity for member departments and agencies to monitor the individual's performance in a tailored program against the eligibility criteria and adjudicative standards when unresolved concerns are present. When an individual is assigned to perform sensitive work requiring access to SCI, the SOIC for the department, agency, or government program to which the individual is assigned will assume security supervision of that individual throughout the period of his or her assignment.

b. The continuing security programs will include the following:

1. Individuals are required to inform the department or agency that grants their SCI access about any personal problem or situation that may have a possible bearing on their eligibility for continued access to SCI and to seek appropriate guidance and assistance. Security guidance should be provided by an official who understands both the eligibility issues involved, and the unique sensitivities of the specific SCI program being supported. As appropriate, tailored monitoring programs should be established to ensure that individuals actively resolve problems which have led to concern about their continued eligibility for access. An individual participating in a monitoring program with a particular department

or agency does not meet the criteria for automatic reciprocal acceptance of SCI eligibility as established by Executive Order 12968. In these situations, each organization should make their own determination of eligibility.

2. SCI security education programs of the member departments and agencies will be established and maintained pursuant to the requirements of Annex E of this directive.

3. Security awareness programs for supervisory personnel will be established and maintained to ensure that supervisory personnel recognize and discharge their special responsibility to safeguard SCI, including the need to assess continued eligibility for SCI access. These programs will provide practical guidance on indicators that may signal matters of security concern. Specific instructions concerning reporting procedures will be disseminated to enable the appropriate authority to take timely corrective action to safeguard the security of the United States as well as to provide all necessary help to the individual concerned to neutralize his or her vulnerability.

4. Security review programs will ensure that appropriate security authorities always receive and exchange, in a timely manner, all information, including lead information, bearing on the security posture of persons having access to SCI. Personal history information will be kept current. Security and related files will be kept under continuing review.

5. Where permitted by agency policy, security review programs may include the use of polygraph examinations conducted by a qualified polygraph examiner.

c. Whenever adverse or derogatory information is discovered or inconsistencies arise that could impact on an individual's security status, appropriate investigation will be conducted on a timely basis. The investigation will be of sufficient scope necessary to resolve the specific adverse or derogatory information or inconsistency in question so that a determination can be made as to whether the individual's continued utilization in activities requiring SCI is clearly consistent with the interest of national security.

13. Implementation.

Existing directives, regulations, agreements, and other guidance governing access to SCI as defined herein will be revised accordingly.

Signed by George D. Tenet   02 July 1998
Director of Central Intelligence   Date

ANNEX A

Investigative Standards for Background Investigations for Access to Classified Information

1. Introduction.

The following investigative standards are established for all United States Government civilian and military personnel, consultants, contractors, employees of contractors, licensees, certificate holders or grantees and their employees and other individuals who require access to classified information, to include Sensitive Compartmented Information (SCI) and Special Access Programs (SAPs), and are to be used by government departments and agencies as the investigative basis for final clearance determinations. However, nothing in these standards prohibits an agency from using any lawful investigative procedures in addition to these requirements in order to resolve any issue identified in the course of a background investigation or reinvestigation.

2. The Three Standards.

There are three standards (Table 1 in the Appendix summarizes when to use each one):

a. The investigation and reinvestigation standards for "L" access authorizations and for access to CONFIDENTIAL and SECRET (including all SECRET-level SAPs not specifically approved for enhanced investigative requirements by an official authorized to establish SAPs by sect. 4.4 of Executive Order 12958);

b. The investigation standard for "Q" access authorizations and for access to TOP SECRET (including TOP SECRET SAPs) and SCI; and

c. The reinvestigation standard for continued access to the levels listed in para. 2(b).

3. Exception to Periods of Coverage.

Some elements of standards specify a period of coverage (e.g., seven years). Where appropriate, such coverage may be shortened to the period from the Subject's eighteenth birthday to the present or to two years, whichever is longer.

4. Expanding Investigations.

Investigations and reinvestigations may be expanded under the provisions of Executive Order 12968 and other applicable statutes and Executive Orders.

5. Transferability.

Investigations that satisfy the requirements of a given standard and are current meet the investigative requirements of all levels specified for the standard. They shall be mutually and reciprocally accepted by all agencies.

6. Breaks in Service.

If a person who requires access has been retired or separated from US Government employment for less than two years and is the Subject of an investigation that is otherwise current, the agency regranting the access will, as a minimum, review an updated Standard Form 86 and applicable records. A reinvestigation is not required unless the review indicates the person may no longer satisfy the standards of Executive Order 12968 (see Table 2).

7. The National Agency Check.

The National Agency Check is part of all investigations and reinvestigations. It consists of a review of:

a. Investigative and criminal history files of the FBI, including a technical fingerprint search;

b. OPM's Security/Suitability Investigations Index;

c. DoD's Defense Clearance and Investigations Index; and

d. Such other national agencies (e.g., CIA, INS) as appropriate to the individual's background.

STANDARD A

National Agency Check with Local Agency Checks and Credit Check (NACLC)

8. Applicability.

Standard A applies to investigations and reinvestigations for:

a. Access to CONFIDENTIAL and SECRET (including all SECRET-level SAPs not specifically approved for enhanced investigative requirements by an official authorized to establish SAPs by sect. 4.4 of Executive Order 12958), and

b. "L" access authorizations.

9. For Reinvestigations: When to Reinvestigate.

The reinvestigation may be initiated at any time following completion of, but not later than ten years (fifteen years for CONFIDENTIAL) from the date of, the previous investigation or reinvestigation. (Table 2 reflects the specific requirements for when to request a reinvestigation, including when there has been a break in service.)

10. Investigative Requirements.

Investigative requirements are as follows:

a. Completion of forms: completion of Standard Form 86, including applicable releases and supporting documentation.

b. National Agency Check: completion of a National Agency Check.

c. Financial Review: verification of the Subject's financial status, including credit bureau checks covering all locations where the Subject has resided, been employed, or attended school for six months or more for the past seven years.

d. Date and Place of Birth: corroboration of date and place of birth through a check of appropriate documentation, if *not* completed in any previous investigation; a check of Bureau of Vital Statistics records when any discrepancy is found to exist.

e. Local Agency Checks: as a minimum, all investigations will include checks of law enforcement agencies having jurisdiction where the Subject has lived, worked, and/or attended school within the last five years, and if applicable, of the appropriate agency for any identified arrests.

11. Expanding the Investigation.

The investigation may be expanded if necessary to determine if access is clearly consistent with the national security.

STANDARD B

Single Scope Background Investigation (SSBI)

12. Applicability.

Standard B applies to initial investigations for:

a. Access to TOP SECRET (including TOP SECRET SAPs) and SCI; and

b. "Q" access authorizations.

13. Investigative Requirements.

Investigative requirements are as follows:

a. Completion of Forms: completion of Standard Form 86, including applicable releases and supporting documentation.

b. National Agency Check: completion of a National Agency Check.

c. National Agency Check for the Spouse or Cohabitant (if applicable): completion of a National Agency Check, without fingerprint cards, for the spouse or cohabitant.

d. Date and Place of Birth: corroboration of date and place of birth through a check of appropriate documentation; a check of Bureau of Vital Statistics records when any discrepancy is found to exist.

e. Citizenship: for individuals born outside the United States, verification of US citizenship directly from the appropriate registration authority; verification of US citizenship or legal status of foreign-born immediate family members (spouse, cohabitant, father, mother, sons, daughters, brothers, sisters).

f. Education: corroboration of most recent or most significant claimed attendance, degree, or diploma. Interviews of appropriate educational sources if education is a primary activity of the Subject during the most recent three years.

g. Employment: verification of all employments for the past seven years; personal interviews of sources (supervisors, coworkers, or both) for each employment of six months or more; corroboration through records or sources of all periods of unemployment exceeding sixty days; verification of all prior federal and military service, including discharge type. For military members, all service within one branch of the armed forces will be considered as one employment, regardless of assignments.

h. References: four references, of whom at least two are developed; to the extent practicable, all should have social knowledge of the Subject and collectively span at least the last seven years.

i. Former Spouse: an interview of any former spouse divorced within the last ten years.

j. Neighborhoods: confirmation of all residences for the last three years through appropriate interviews with neighbors and through records reviews.

k. Financial Review: verification of the Subject's financial status, including credit bureau checks covering all locations where Subject has resided, been employed, and/or attended school for six months or more for the last seven years.

l. Local Agency Checks: a check of appropriate criminal history records covering all locations where, for the last ten years, the Subject has resided, been employed, and/or attended school for six months or more, including current residence regardless of duration. (NOTE: If no residence, employment or education exceeds six months, local agency checks should be performed as deemed appropriate.)

m. Public Records: verification of divorces, bankruptcies, and other court actions, whether civil or criminal, involving the Subject.

n. Subject Interview: a Subject Interview, conducted by trained security, investigative, or counterintelligence personnel. During the investigation, additional Subject Interviews may be conducted to collect relevant information, to resolve significant inconsistencies, or both. Sworn statements and unsworn declarations may be taken whenever appropriate.

o. Polygraph (only agencies with approved personnel security polygraph programs): in departments or agencies with policies sanctioning the use of the polygraph for personnel security purposes, the investigation may include a polygraph examination, conducted by a qualified polygraph examiner.

14. Expanding the Investigation.

The investigation may be expanded as necessary. As appropriate, interviews with anyone able to provide information or to resolve issues, including but not limited to cohabitants, relatives, psychiatrists, psychologists, other medical professional, and law enforcement professionals may be conducted.

STANDARD C
Single-Scope Background Investigation-Periodic Reinvestigation (SSBI-PR)

15. Applicability.

Standard C applies to reinvestigations for:

    a. Access to TOP SECRET (including TOP SECRET SAPs) and SCI; and

    b. "Q" access authorizations.

16. When to Reinvestigate.

The reinvestigation may be initiated at any time following completion of, but not later than five years from date of, the previous investigation (see Table 2).

17. Reinvestigative Requirements.

Reinvestigative requirements are as follows:

    a. Completion of Forms: completion of Standard Form 86, including applicable releases and supporting documentation.

    b. National Agency Check: completion of a National Agency Check (fingerprint cards are required *only* if there has not been a previous valid technical check of the FBI).

    c. National Agency Check for the Spouse or Cohabitant (if applicable): completion of a National Agency Check, without fingerprint cards, for the spouse or cohabitant. The National Agency Check for the spouse or cohabitant is *not* required if already completed in conjunction with a previous investigation or reinvestigation.

    d. Employment: verification of all employments since the last investigation. Attempts to interview a sufficient number of sources (supervisors, coworkers, or both) at all employments of six months or more. For military members, all service within one branch of the armed forces will be considered as one employment, regardless of assignments.

    e. References: interviews with two character references who are knowledgeable of the Subject; at least one will be a developed reference. To the extent practical, both should have social knowledge of the Subject and collectively span the entire period of the investigation. As appropriate, additional interviews may be conducted, including with cohabitants and relatives.

    f. Neighborhoods: interviews of two neighbors in the vicinity of the Subject's most recent residence of six months or more. Confirmation of current residence regardless of length.

    g. Financial Review:

        1. Financial Status: verification of the Subject's financial status, including credit bureau checks covering all locations where Subject has resided, been employed, and/or attended school for six months or more for the period covered by the

reinvestigation;

2. Check of Treasury's Financial Database: Agencies may request the Department of the Treasury, under terms and conditions prescribed by the Secretary of the Treasury, to search automated databases consisting of reports of currency transactions by financial institutions, international transportation of currency or monetary instruments, foreign bank and financial accounts, and transactions under $10,000 that are reported as possible money laundering violations.

h. Local Agency Checks: a check of appropriate criminal history records covering all locations where, during the period covered by the reinvestigation, the Subject has resided, been employed, and/or attended school for six months or more, including current residence regardless of duration. (NOTE: If no residence, employment, or education exceeds six months, local agency checks should be performed as deemed appropriate.)

i. Former Spouse: an interview with any former spouse unless the divorce took place before the date of the last investigation or reinvestigation.

j. Public Records: verification of divorces, bankruptcies, and other court actions, whether civil or criminal, involving the Subject since the date of the last investigation.

k. Subject Interviews: a Subject Interview, conducted by trained security, investigative, or counterintelligence personnel. During the reinvestigation, additional Subject Interviews may be conducted to collect relevant information, to resolve significant inconsistencies, or both. Sworn statements and unsworn declarations may be taken whenever appropriate.

18. Expanding the Reinvestigation.

The reinvestigation may be expanded as necessary. As appropriate, interviews with anyone able to provide information or to resolve issues, including but not limited to cohabitants, relatives, psychiatrists, psychologists, other medical professionals, and law enforcement professionals may be conducted.

Appendix

Decision Tables

TABLE 1: WHICH INVESTIGATION TO REQUEST

If the requirement is for	And the person has this access	Based on this investigation	Then the investigation required is	Using standard
CONFIDENTIAL SECRET; "L"	none CONF,SEC;"L"	none out of date NACLC or SSBI	NACLC	A
TOP SECRET, QSI; "Q"	none none; CONF, SEC; "L" TS, SCI; "Q"	none current or out of date NACLC out of date SSBI	SSBI SSBI-PR	B C

TABLE 2: REINVESTIGATION REQUIREMENTS

If the requirement is for	And the age of the investigation is	Type required if there has been a break in service of ____	
		0-23 months	24 months or more
CONFIDENTIAL	0 to 14 yrs. 11 mos.	none (NOTE 1)	NACLC
	15 yrs. Or more	NACLC	
SECRET; "L"	0 to 9 yrs. 11 mos.	none (NOTE 1)	
	10 yrs. Or more	NACLC	
TOP SECRET, SCI; "Q"	0 to 4 yrs. 11 mos.	none (NOTE 1)	SSBI
		SSBI-PR	
	5 yrs. Or more		

NOTE 1: As a minimum, review an updated Std. Fm. 86 and applicable records. A reinvestigation (NACLC or SSBI-PR) is not required unless the review indicates the person may no longer satisfy the standards of Executive Order 12968.

DCID 6/4

Investigative Standards for Temporary Eligibility for Access

1. Introduction.

The following minimum investigative standards, implementing section 3.3 of Executive Order 12968, "Access to Classified Information", are established for all United States Government and military personnel, consultants, contractors, subcontractors, employees of contractors, licensees, certificate holders or grantees and their employees and other individuals who require access to classified information before the appropriate investigation can be completed and a final determination made.

2. Temporary Eligibility for Access.

Based on a justified need meeting the requirements of section 3.3 of Executive Order 12968, temporary eligibility for access may be granted before investigations are complete and favorably adjudicated, where official functions must be performed prior to completion of the investigation and adjudication process. The temporary eligibility will be valid until completion of the investigation and adjudication; however, the agency granting it may revoke it at any time based on unfavorable information identified in the course of the investigation.

3. Temporary Eligibility for Access at the CONFIDENTIAL and SECRET Levels and Temporary Eligibility for "L" Access Authorization.

As a minimum, such temporary eligibility requires completion of the Standard Form 86, including any applicable supporting documentation, favorable review of the form by the appropriate adjudicating authority, and submission of a request for an expedited National Agency Check with Local Agency Checks and Credit (NACLC).

4. Temporary Eligibility for Access at the TOP SECRET and SCI Levels and Temporary Eligibility for "Q" Access Authorization: For Someone who is the Subject of a Favorable Investigation not Meeting the Investigative Standards for Access at those Levels.

As a minimum, such temporary eligibility requires completion of the Standard Form 86, including any applicable supporting documentation, favorable review of the form by the appropriate adjudicating authority, and expedited submission of a request for a Single Scope Background Investigation (SSBI).

5. Temporary Eligibility for Access at the TOP SECRET and SCI Levels and Temporary Eligibility for "Q" Access Authorization: For Someone who is not the Subject of a current, favorable personnel or Personnel Security Investigation of any kind.

As a minimum, such temporary eligibility requires completion of the Standard Form 86, including any applicable supporting documentation, favorable review of the form by the appropriate adjudicating authority, immediate submission of a request for an expedited SSBI, and completion and favorable review by the appropriate adjudicating authority of relevant criminal history and investigative records of the Federal Bureau of Investigation and of information in the Security/Suitability Investigations Index (SII) and the Defense Clearance and Investigations Index (DCII).

6. Additional Requirements by Agencies.

Temporary eligibility for access must satisfy these minimum investigations standards, but agency heads may establish additional requirements based on the sensitivity of the particular, identified categories of classified information necessary to perform the lawful and authorized functions that are the basis for granting temporary eligibility for access. However, no additional requirements shall exceed the common standards for background investigations developed under section 3.2(b) of Executive Order 12968. Temporary eligibility for access is valid only at the agency granting it and at other agencies who expressly agree to accept it and acknowledge understanding of its investigative basis. It is further subject to limitations specified in sections 2.4(d) and 3.3 of Executive Order 12968, "Access to Classified Information."

ANNEX B

Quality Control Guidelines for the Single Scope Background Investigation

1. Guidelines.

In accordance with the requirements of DCID 6/4 , this document sets out guidelines to maintain quality standards for the Single Scope Background Investigation (SSBI). These guidelines assume the adjudicator's perspective because the adjudicator is the ultimate customer for the SSBI. The guidelines are divided into:

- Definition of Quality

- Conduct of the Interview

- Collection Requirements (Coverage)

- Quality Control Activities.

SOICs will ensure that investigative personnel employed by or assigned or detailed to their agencies/departments receive adequate initial and ongoing training in investigation and interrogation techniques, as well as familiarization with counterintelligence issues that may arise during investigation. Training should also incorporate findings of contemporary research in personnel security and medical disciplines and, in addition, evolving legal issues that may impact investigation collection requirements. As much as possible, training should be conducted as a joint effort with other investigative entities supporting the Intelligence Community, to facilitate information sharing and to enhance reciprocity.

2. Definition of Quality.

A quality investigation is a thorough and comprehensive collection of favorable and unfavorable information from a variety of sources, past and present, that may include employment(s), reference(s), neighborhood(s), credit, police, and the Subject.

The determination of eligibility for access to sensitive compartmented information is a discretionary determination using the whole person concept that such access is clearly in the interests of the national security. Accordingly, the investigation will be comprehensive and in such detail so as to affirmatively address unquestioned loyalty to the United States, strength of character, trustworthiness, honesty, reliability, discretion, and sound judgment, as well as freedom from conflicting allegiances and potential for coercion, and willingness and ability to abide by regulations governing the use, handling and protection of sensitive compartmented information.

3. Conduct of the Interview

The quality of the investigation depends on the investigator's ability to elicit information from a source knowledgeable about the Subject. This is basic to the conduct of any interview. The investigator should plan and execute each interview so as to obtain the maximum amount of information from a source. Available sources should be selected from each area of coverage to ensure that pertinent information about the Subject's entire background is developed.

The investigator should conduct the interview in person and find a suitable location that protects privacy. Telephonic interviews are strongly discouraged; however, occasionally exigent circumstances may dictate that the interviews be conducted by telephone. If a telephonic interview is necessary, the report should always state why the interview was not conducted in person.

The investigator should initially advise the source of the reason/purpose for the investigation and should attempt to establish a degree of confidence in the source(s) that will promote a high level of rapport and cooperation.

The investigator should also advise the source about the Privacy Act of 1974, before completing the interview, since the source needs to understand that the Subject of the investigation has the right to review information provided by a source and has the right to know a source's identity, unless the source requests confidentiality.

4. Collection Requirement (Coverage)

  a. For all Sources.
      Investigators should establish the duration and nature of association between the source and the Subject to assess the source's extent of knowledge. The investigator should always secure the source's full name and any other appropriate identifying data, particularly in the case of a source with a common name. All derogatory or noteworthy information concerning the Subject of the investigation that is provided by a source should be fully explored in the interview, including elicitation of the names of any corroborating sources or record information that will substantiate any derogatory testimony provided by the source. For all sources, the report should indicate what issue areas were covered and whether the information provided was favorable or unfavorable.

  b. For References and Neighbors.
      Depending on the source's degree of association, investigators should ask each reference or neighbor relevant information regarding the Subject's:

      1. Family, citizenship, education, employment, residence history, and military service.

      2. Reputation, character, honesty, trustworthiness, integrity, discretion, reliability, and temperament.

      3. Financial stability, organizational affiliations, and whether there is a history of mental, emotional, or physical health problems.

      4. Whether the Subject exhibits a pattern of excessive use of alcohol or has ever used illegal drugs or abused prescription drugs.

      5. Activities which indicate a lack of discretion or demonstrate poor judgment, a character flaw, or a personality disorder.

6. Participation in criminal activity or an altercation with law enforcement agencies.

7. Travels abroad for business or pleasure and degree of contact with foreign nationals.

8. Unquestioned loyalty to the United States.

If a Subject has had access to classified information and a source is in a position to know, the investigator should ask whether the Subject properly handles classified information or has ever had a security violation. Finally, the investigator should ask if the source can recommend the Subject for a position of trust and responsibility with the US Government or, in the case of a contractor, can the Subject be trusted with classified information. The investigator should conclude the interview by asking the source to provide names of additional references.

c. Follow-up Questions.
If a source provides noteworthy or derogatory information to questions in any of the above areas of consideration, the investigator should ask follow-up questions as necessary to elicit all available information. The investigator should report as fully as possible:

1. The nature, extent, and seriousness of the conduct.

2. The motivation for and the circumstances surrounding the conduct.

3. The frequency and recency of the conduct.

4. The Subject's age and maturity at the time of the conduct.

5. Whether the conduct was voluntary or whether there was pressure, coercion, or exploitation leading to the conduct.

6. Whether the Subject has been rehabilitated or has exhibited other pertinent behavioral changes since the conduct.

If the Subject has ended the questionable conduct, the investigator should attempt to determine the motivation for positive change. The investigator should also attempt to establish whether there may be personal animosity or bias towards the Subject on the part of the source(s). The investigator should supply any available documentary evidence relating to the conduct in addition to the report of the source.

d. For Employment References.
The investigator should identify and interview the best source(s) available. These employment references should include, but are not limited to, the Subject's immediate supervisor, coworker(s), and other persons with frequent professional contact. Where appropriate, the investigator should pursue the same line of inquiry as with references and neighbors. In particular, the investigator should inquire regarding:

1. Whether the Subject is willing to abide by company policies and regulations.

2. Whether the Subject appropriately safeguards the employer's proprietary/sensitive information.

3. Whether the Subject is financially stable.

4. Whether the Subject has a history of substance abuse, to include alcohol, and/or prescription drugs.

5. Whether the Subject has been involved in any criminal activity.

6. Whether the Subject is reliable and eligible for re-hire.

The investigator should obtain any available documentary evidence to support the report of the source(s).

e. For Subject Interviews.
The Subject is the best source of information about himself/herself. Hence, the investigator should explore with the Subject the same line of inquiry she/he pursues with a reference, neighborhood, and employment source(s). The investigator should obtain the Subject's version of the details surrounding all issues arising either in the course of the interview or in other parts of the investigation that have been completed by the time of the Subject Interview and report them completely. The investigator should inquire regarding:

1. What happened and why.

2. Where, when, how, and how often it happened.

3. Who else was involved.

4. Was the conduct voluntary.

Of particular value to the adjudicator is evidence that the Subject is being contradictory or dissembling. If the Subject claims to have ended the conduct, the investigator should attempt to determine the motivation for positive change. The investigator should report only the facts.

5. Quality Control Activities.

Quality control activities are designed to ensure that a high quality investigation and report have been provided. The following management tools can be used by investigative agencies to ensure quality investigations, and other techniques may be appropriate:

a. Case Review.
Case review consists of a supervisory review of the investigative requirements and the investigation to ensure that all coverage has been met using the best available sources. Depending on the agency, the investigative review may be conducted by the investigator's supervisor or by a quality assurance or assessment team.

b. Ride-Along Program.
In ride-along programs, supervisors and/or senior agents accompany the investigator, observing the investigator's performance, focusing on whether the investigator:

1. Uses proper/acceptable investigative techniques.

2. Explores all relevant issues.

3. Possesses a demeanor that reflects positively on the investigative agency.

c. Source Recontact.
The supervisory element may select from a sample of an investigator's cases and contact some or all of the sources. The source is queried regarding the investigator's professionalism, line of questioning, adherence to established policies and procedures, and thoroughness. Both written and telephonic re-contact are acceptable.

These recommended monitoring activities ensure adequate training of investigators, acceptable supervisory oversight, and proper professionalism while conducting the investigation. They also ensure that the standards of investigative coverage are satisfactorily met.

THE WHITE HOUSE

WASHINGTON

December 29, 2005

MEMORANDUM FOR WILLIAM LEONARD
                Director
                Information Security Oversight Office

SUBJECT: Adjudicative Guidelines

The President has approved the attached revision of the
Adjudicative Guidelines for Determining Eligibility for Access to
Classified Information as recommended unanimously by the NSC's
PCC on Records Access and Information Security. Please circulate
the revised guidelines to all affected agencies for immediate
implementation. It is important to emphasize that all agencies
must honor clearances granted under these guidelines, consistent
with Executive Order 12968 and the December 12, 2005 memorandum
to agencies from OMB Deputy Director for Management Clay Johnson.

Stephen J. Hadley
Assistant to the President
    for National Security Affairs

Attachment
Tab A   Revised Adjudicative Guidelines for Determining
           Eligibility for Access to Classified Information

Adjudicative Guidelines for Determining Eligibility
For Access to Classified Information

1. *Introduction.* The following adjudicative guidelines are established for all U.S. government civilian and military personnel, consultants, contractors, employees of contractors, licensees, certificate holders or grantees and their employees, and other individuals who require access to classified information. They apply to persons being considered for initial or continued eligibility for access to classified information, to include sensitive compartmented information and special access programs, and are to be used by government departments and agencies in all final clearance determinations. Government departments and agencies may also choose to apply these guidelines to analogous situations regarding persons being considered for access to other types of protected information.

Decisions regarding eligibility for access to classified information take into account factors that could cause a conflict of interest and place a person in the position of having to choose between his or her commitments to the United States, including the commitment to protect classified information, and any other compelling loyalty. Access decisions also take into account a person's reliability, trustworthiness and ability to protect classified information. No coercive policing could replace the self-discipline and integrity of the person entrusted with the nation's secrets as the most effective means of protecting them. When a person's life history shows evidence of unreliability or untrustworthiness, questions arise whether the person can be relied on and trusted to exercise the responsibility necessary for working in a secure environment where protecting classified information is paramount.

2. *The Adjudicative Process.*

(a) The adjudicative process is an examination of a sufficient period of a person's life to make an affirmative determination that the person is an acceptable security risk. Eligibility for access to classified information is predicated upon the individual meeting these personnel security guidelines. The adjudication process is the careful weighing of a number of variables known as the whole-person concept. Available, reliable information about the person, past and present, favorable and unfavorable, should be considered in reaching a determination. In evaluating the relevance of an individual's conduct, the adjudicator should consider the following factors:

(1) the nature, extent, and seriousness of the conduct;

(2) the circumstances surrounding the conduct, to include knowledgeable participation;

(3) the frequency and recency of the conduct;

(4) the individual's age and maturity at the time of the conduct;

(5) the extent to which participation is voluntary;

(6) the presence or absence of rehabilitation and other permanent behavioral changes;

(7) the motivation for the conduct;

(8) the potential for pressure, coercion, exploitation, or duress; and

(9) the likelihood of continuation or recurrence;

(b) Each case must be judged on its own merits, and final determination remains the responsibility of the specific department or agency. Any doubt concerning personnel being considered for access to classified information will be resolved in favor of the national security.

(c) The ability to develop specific thresholds for action under these guidelines is limited by the nature and complexity of human behavior. The ultimate determination of whether the granting or continuing of eligibility for a security clearance is clearly consistent with the interests of national security must be an overall common sense judgment based upon careful consideration of the following guidelines, each of which is to be evaluated in the context of the whole person.

(1) GUIDELINE A: Allegiance to the United States;

(2) GUIDELINE B: Foreign Influence

(3) GUIDELINE C: Foreign Preference;

(4) GUIDELINE D: Sexual Behavior;

(5) GUIDELINE E: Personal Conduct;

(6) GUIDELINE F: Financial Considerations;

(7) GUIDELINE G: Alcohol Consumption;

(8) GUIDELINE H: Drug Involvement;

(9) GUIDELINE I: Psychological Conditions;

(10) GUIDELINE J: Criminal Conduct;

(11) GUIDELINE K: Handling Protected Information;

(12) GUIDELINE L: Outside Activities;

(13) GUIDELINE M: Use of Information Technology Systems

(d) Although adverse information concerning a single criterion may not be sufficient for an unfavorable determination, the individual may be disqualified if available information reflects a recent or recurring pattern of questionable judgment, irresponsibility, or emotionally unstable behavior. Notwithstanding the whole-person concept, pursuit of further investigation may be terminated by an appropriate adjudicative agency in the face of reliable, significant, disqualifying, adverse information.

(e) When information of security concern becomes known about an individual who is currently eligible for access to classified information, the adjudicator should consider whether the person:

(1) voluntarily reported the information;

(2) was truthful and complete in responding to questions;

(3) sought assistance and followed professional guidance, where appropriate;

(4) resolved or appears likely to favorably resolve the security concern;

(5) has demonstrated positive changes in behavior and employment;

(6) should have his or her access temporarily suspended pending final adjudication of the information.

(f) If after evaluating information of security concern, the adjudicator decides that the information is not serious enough to warrant a recommendation of disapproval or revocation of the security clearance, it may be appropriate to recommend approval with a warning that future incidents of a similar nature may result in revocation of access.

GUIDELINE A: ALLEGIANCE TO THE UNITED STATES

3. *The Concern.* An individual must be of unquestioned allegiance to the United States. The willingness to safeguard classified information is in doubt if there is any reason to suspect an individual's allegiance to the United States.

4. *Conditions that could raise a security concern and may be disqualifying include:*

(a) involvement in, support of, training to commit, or advocacy of any act of sabotage, espionage, treason, terrorism, or sedition against the United States of America;

(b) association or sympathy with persons who are attempting to commit, or who are committing, any of the above acts;

(c) association or sympathy with persons or organizations that advocate, threaten, or use force or violence, or use any other illegal or unconstitutional means, in an effort to:

(1) overthrow or influence the government of the United States or any state or local government;

(2) prevent Federal, state, or local government personnel from performing their official duties;

(3) gain retribution for perceived wrongs caused by the Federal, state, or local government;

(4) prevent others from exercising their rights under the Constitution or laws of the United States or of any state.

5. *Conditions that could mitigate security concerns include:*

(a) the individual was unaware of the unlawful aims of the individual or organization and severed ties upon learning of these;

(b) the individual's involvement was only with the lawful or humanitarian aspects of such an organization;

(c) involvement in the above activities occurred for only a short period of time and was attributable to curiosity or academic interest;

(d) the involvement or association with such activities occurred under such unusual circumstances, or so much time has elapsed, that it is unlikely to recur and does not cast doubt on the individual's current reliability, trustworthiness, or loyalty.

GUIDELINE B: FOREIGN INFLUENCE

6. *The Concern.* Foreign contacts and interests may be a security concern if the individual has divided loyalties or foreign financial interests, may be manipulated or induced to help a foreign person, group, organization, or government in a way that is not in U.S. interests, or is vulnerable to pressure or coercion by any foreign interest. Adjudication under this Guideline can and should consider the identity of the foreign country in which the foreign contact or financial interest is located, including, but not limited to, such considerations as whether the foreign country is known to target United States citizens to obtain protected information and/or is associated with a risk of terrorism.

7. *Conditions that could raise a security concern and may be disqualifying include:*

(a) contact with a foreign family member, business or professional associate, friend, or other person who is a citizen of or resident in a foreign country if that contact creates a heightened risk of foreign exploitation, inducement, manipulation, pressure, or coercion;

(b) connections to a foreign person, group, government, or country that create a potential conflict of interest between the individual's obligation to protect sensitive information or technology and the individual's desire to help a foreign person, group, or country by providing that information;

(c) counterintelligence information, that may be classified, indicates that the individual's access to protected information may involve unacceptable risk to national security;

(d) sharing living quarters with a person or persons, regardless of citizenship status, if that relationship creates a heightened risk of foreign inducement, manipulation, pressure, or coercion;

(e) a substantial business, financial, or property interest in a foreign country, or in any foreign-owned or foreign-operated business, which could subject the individual to heightened risk of foreign influence or exploitation;

(f) failure to report, when required, association with a foreign national;

(g) unauthorized association with a suspected or known agent, associate, or employee of a foreign intelligence service;

(h) indications that representatives or nationals from a foreign country are acting to increase the vulnerability of the individual to possible future exploitation, inducement, manipulation, pressure, or coercion;

(i) conduct, especially while traveling outside the U.S., which may make the individual vulnerable to exploitation, pressure, or coercion by a foreign person, group, government, or country.

8. *Conditions that could mitigate security concerns include:*

(a) the nature of the relationships with foreign persons, the country in which these persons are located, or the positions or activities of those persons in that country are such that it is unlikely the individual will be placed in a position of having to choose between the interests of a foreign individual, group, organization, or government and the interests of the U.S.;

(b) there is no conflict of interest, either because the individual's sense of loyalty or obligation to the foreign person, group, government, or country is so minimal, or the individual has such deep and longstanding relationships and loyalties in the U.S., that the individual can be expected to resolve any conflict of interest in favor of the U.S. interest;

(c) contact or communication with foreign citizens is so casual and infrequent that there is little likelihood that it could create a risk for foreign influence or exploitation;

(d) the foreign contacts and activities are on U.S. Government business or are approved by the cognizant security authority;

(e) the individual has promptly complied with existing agency requirements regarding the reporting of contacts, requests, or threats from persons, groups, or organizations from a foreign country;

(f) the value or routine nature of the foreign business, financial, or property interests is such that they are unlikely to result in a conflict and could not be used effectively to influence, manipulate, or pressure the individual.

GUIDELINE C: FOREIGN PREFERENCE

9. *The Concern.* When an individual acts in such a way as to indicate a preference for a foreign country over the United States, then he or she may be prone to provide information or make decisions that are harmful to the interests of the United States.

10. *Conditions that could raise a security concern and may be disqualifying include:*

(a) exercise of any right, privilege or obligation of foreign citizenship after becoming a U.S. citizen or through the foreign citizenship of a family member. This includes but is not limited to:

(1) possession of a current foreign passport;

(2) military service or a willingness to bear arms for a foreign country;

(3) accepting educational, medical, retirement, social welfare, or other such benefits from a foreign country;

(4) residence in a foreign country to meet citizenship requirements;

(5) using foreign citizenship to protect financial or business interests in another country;

(6) seeking or holding political office in a foreign country;

(7) voting in a foreign election;

(b) action to acquire or obtain recognition of a foreign citizenship by an American citizen;

(c) performing or attempting to perform duties, or otherwise acting, so as to serve the interests of a foreign person, group, organization, or government in conflict with the national security interest;

(d) any statement or action that shows allegiance to a country other than the United States: for example, declaration of intent to renounce United States citizenship; renunciation of United States citizenship.

11. *Conditions that could mitigate security concerns include:*

(a) dual citizenship is based solely on parents' citizenship or birth in a foreign country;

(b) the individual has expressed a willingness to renounce dual citizenship;

(c) exercise of the rights, privileges, or obligations of foreign citizenship occurred before the individual became a U.S. citizen or when the individual was a minor;

(d) use of a foreign passport is approved by the cognizant security authority;

(e) the passport has been destroyed, surrendered to the cognizant security authority, or otherwise invalidated;

(f) the vote in a foreign election was encouraged by the United States Government.

GUIDELINE D: SEXUAL BEHAVIOR

12. *The Concern.* Sexual behavior that involves a criminal offense, indicates a personality or emotional disorder, reflects lack of judgment or discretion, or which may subject the individual to undue influence or coercion, exploitation, or duress can raise questions about an individual's reliability, trustworthiness and ability to protect classified information. No adverse inference concerning the standards in this Guideline may be raised solely on the basis of the sexual orientation of the individual.

13. *Conditions that could raise a security concern and may be disqualifying include:*

(a) sexual behavior of a criminal nature, whether or not the individual has been prosecuted;

(b) a pattern of compulsive, self-destructive, or high risk sexual behavior that the person is unable to stop or that may be symptomatic of a personality disorder;

(c) sexual behavior that causes an individual to be vulnerable to coercion, exploitation, or duress;

(d) sexual behavior of a public nature and/or that reflects lack of discretion or judgment.

14. *Conditions that could mitigate security concerns include:*

(a) the behavior occurred prior to or during adolescence and there is no evidence of subsequent conduct of a similar nature;

(b) the sexual behavior happened so long ago, so infrequently, or under such unusual circumstances, that it is unlikely to recur and does not cast doubt on the individual's current reliability, trustworthiness, or good judgment;

(c) the behavior no longer serves as a basis for coercion, exploitation, or duress.

(d) the sexual behavior is strictly private, consensual, and discreet.

GUIDELINE E: PERSONAL CONDUCT

15. *The Concern.* Conduct involving questionable judgment, lack of candor, dishonesty, or unwillingness to comply with rules and regulations can raise questions about an individual's reliability, trustworthiness and ability to protect classified information. Of special interest is any failure to provide truthful and candid answers during the security clearance process or any other failure to cooperate with the security clearance process.

The following will normally result in an unfavorable clearance action or administrative termination of further processing for clearance eligibility:

(a) refusal, or failure without reasonable cause, to undergo or cooperate with security processing, including but not limited to meeting with a security investigator for subject interview, completing security forms or releases, and cooperation with medical or psychological evaluation;

(b) refusal to provide full, frank and truthful answers to lawful questions of investigators, security officials, or other official representatives in connection with a personnel security or trustworthiness determination.

16. *Conditions that could raise a security concern and may be disqualifying include*

(a) deliberate omission, concealment, or falsification of relevant facts from any personnel security questionnaire, personal history statement, or similar form used to conduct investigations, determine employment qualifications, award benefits or status, determine security clearance eligibility or trustworthiness, or award fiduciary responsibilities;

(b) deliberately providing false or misleading information concerning relevant facts to an employer, investigator, security official, competent medical authority, or other official government representative;

(c) credible adverse information in several adjudicative issue areas that is not sufficient for an adverse determination under any other single guideline, but which, when considered as a whole, supports a whole-person assessment of questionable judgment, untrustworthiness, unreliability, lack of candor, unwillingness to comply with rules and regulations, or other characteristics indicating that the person may not properly safeguard protected information;

(d) credible adverse information that is not explicitly covered under any other guideline and may not be sufficient by itself for an adverse determination, but which, when combined with all available information supports a whole-person assessment of questionable judgment, untrustworthiness, unreliability, lack of candor, unwillingness to comply with rules and regulations, or other characteristics indicating that the person may not properly safeguard protected information. This includes but is not limited to consideration of:

> (1) untrustworthy or unreliable behavior to include breach of client confidentiality, release of proprietary information, unauthorized release of sensitive corporate or other government protected information;

> (2) disruptive, violent, or other inappropriate behavior in the workplace;

> (3) a pattern of dishonesty or rule violations;

> (4) evidence of significant misuse of Government or other employer's time or resources;

(e) personal conduct, or concealment of information about one's conduct, that creates a vulnerability to exploitation, manipulation, or duress, such as (1) engaging in activities which, if known, may affect the person's personal, professional, or community standing, or (2) while in another country, engaging in any activity that is illegal in that country or that is legal in that country but illegal in the United States and may serve as a basis for exploitation or pressure by the foreign security or intelligence service or other group;

(f) violation of a written or recorded commitment made by the individual to the employer as a condition of employment;

(g) association with persons involved in criminal activity.

17. *Conditions that could mitigate security concerns include:*

(a) the individual made prompt, good-faith efforts to correct the omission, concealment, or falsification before being confronted with the facts;

(b) the refusal or failure to cooperate, omission, or concealment was caused or significantly contributed to by improper or inadequate advice of authorized personnel or legal counsel advising or instructing the individual specifically concerning the security clearance process. Upon being made aware of the requirement to cooperate or provide the information, the individual cooperated fully and truthfully.

(c) the offense is so minor, or so much time has passed, or the behavior is so infrequent, or it happened under such unique circumstances that it is unlikely to recur and does not cast doubt on the individual's reliability, trustworthiness, or good judgment;

(d) the individual has acknowledged the behavior and obtained counseling to change the behavior or taken other positive steps to alleviate the stressors, circumstances, or factors that caused untrustworthy, unreliable, or other inappropriate behavior, and such behavior is unlikely to recur;

(e) the individual has taken positive steps to reduce or eliminate vulnerability to exploitation, manipulation, or duress;

(f) the information was unsubstantiated or from a source of questionable reliability;

(g) association with persons involved in criminal activity has ceased or occurs under circumstances that do not cast doubt upon the individual's reliability, trustworthiness, judgment, or willingness to comply with rules and regulations.

GUIDELINE F: FINANCIAL CONSIDERATIONS

18. *The Concern.* Failure or inability to live within one's means, satisfy debts, and meet financial obligations may indicate poor self-control, lack of judgment, or unwillingness to abide by rules and regulations, all of which can raise questions about an individual's reliability, trustworthiness and ability to protect classified information. An individual who is financially overextended is at risk of having to engage in illegal acts to generate funds. Compulsive gambling is a concern as it may lead to financial crimes including espionage. Affluence that cannot be explained by known sources of income is also a security concern. It may indicate proceeds from financially profitable criminal acts.

19. *Conditions that could raise a security concern and may be disqualifying include:*

(a) inability or unwillingness to satisfy debts;

(b) indebtedness caused by frivolous or irresponsible spending and the absence of any evidence of willingness or intent to pay the debt or establish a realistic plan to pay the debt.

(c) a history of not meeting financial obligations;

(d) deceptive or illegal financial practices such as embezzlement, employee theft, check fraud, income tax evasion, expense account fraud, filing deceptive loan statements, and other intentional financial breaches of trust;

(e) consistent spending beyond one's means, which may be indicated by excessive indebtedness, significant negative cash flow, high debt-to-income ratio, and/or other financial analysis;

(f) financial problems that are linked to drug abuse, alcoholism, gambling problems, or other issues of security concern;

(g) failure to file annual Federal, state, or local income tax returns as required or the fraudulent filing of the same;

(h) unexplained affluence, as shown by a lifestyle or standard of living, increase in net worth, or money transfers that cannot be explained by subject's known legal sources of income;

(i) compulsive or addictive gambling as indicated by an unsuccessful attempt to stop gambling, "chasing losses" (i.e. increasing the bets or returning another day in an effort to get even), concealment of gambling losses, borrowing money to fund gambling or pay gambling debts, family conflict or other problems caused by gambling.

20. *Conditions that could mitigate security concerns include*:

(a) the behavior happened so long ago, was so infrequent, or occurred under such circumstances that it is unlikely to recur and does not cast doubt on the individual's current reliability, trustworthiness, or good judgment;

(b) the conditions that resulted in the financial problem were largely beyond the person's control (e.g., loss of employment, a business downturn, unexpected medical emergency, or a death, divorce or separation), and the individual acted responsibly under the circumstances;

(c) the person has received or is receiving counseling for the problem and/or there are clear indications that the problem is being resolved or is under control;

(d) the individual initiated a good-faith effort to repay overdue creditors or otherwise resolve debts;

(e) the individual has a reasonable basis to dispute the legitimacy of the past-due debt which is the cause of the problem and provides documented proof to substantiate the basis of the dispute or provides evidence of actions to resolve the issue;

(f) the affluence resulted from a legal source of income.

GUIDELINE G: ALCOHOL CONSUMPTION

21. *The Concern*. Excessive alcohol consumption often leads to the exercise of questionable judgment or the failure to control impulses, and can raise questions about an individual's reliability and trustworthiness.

22. *Conditions that could raise a security concern and may be disqualifying include*:

(a) alcohol-related incidents away from work, such as driving while under the influence, fighting, child or spouse abuse, disturbing the peace, or other incidents of concern, regardless of whether the individual is diagnosed as an alcohol abuser or alcohol dependent;

(b) alcohol-related incidents at work, such as reporting for work or duty in an intoxicated or impaired condition, or drinking on the job, regardless of whether the individual is diagnosed as an alcohol abuser or alcohol dependent;

(c) habitual or binge consumption of alcohol to the point of impaired judgment, regardless of whether the individual is diagnosed as an alcohol abuser or alcohol dependent;

(d) diagnosis by a duly qualified medical professional (e.g., physician, clinical psychologist, or psychiatrist) of alcohol abuse or alcohol dependence;

(e) evaluation of alcohol abuse or alcohol dependence by a licensed clinical social worker who is a staff member of a recognized alcohol treatment program;

(f) relapse after diagnosis of alcohol abuse or dependence and completion of an alcohol rehabilitation program;

(g) failure to follow any court order regarding alcohol education, evaluation, treatment, or abstinence.

23. *Conditions that could mitigate security concerns include*:

(a) so much time has passed, or the behavior was so infrequent, or it happened under such unusual circumstances that it is unlikely to recur or does not cast doubt on the individual's current reliability, trustworthiness, or good judgment;

(b) the individual acknowledges his or her alcoholism or issues of alcohol abuse, provides evidence of actions taken to overcome this problem, and has established a pattern of abstinence (if alcohol dependent) or responsible use (if an alcohol abuser);

(c) the individual is a current employee who is participating in a counseling or treatment program, has no history of previous treatment and relapse, and is making satisfactory progress;

(d) the individual has successfully completed inpatient or outpatient counseling or rehabilitation along with any required aftercare, has demonstrated a clear and established pattern of modified consumption or abstinence in accordance with treatment recommendations, such as participation in meetings of Alcoholics Anonymous or a similar organization and has received a favorable prognosis by a duly qualified medical professional or a licensed clinical social worker who is a staff member of a recognized alcohol treatment program.

GUIDELINE H: DRUG INVOLVEMENT

24. *The Concern*. Use of an illegal drug or misuse of a prescription drug can raise questions about an individual's reliability and trustworthiness, both because it may impair judgment and because it raises questions about a person's ability or willingness to comply with laws, rules, and regulations.

(a) Drugs are defined as mood and behavior altering substances, and include:

(1) Drugs, materials, and other chemical compounds identified and listed in the Controlled Substances Act of 1970, as amended (e.g., marijuana or cannabis, depressants, narcotics, stimulants, and hallucinogens), and

(2) inhalants and other similar substances;

(b) drug abuse is the illegal use of a drug or use of a legal drug in a manner that deviates from approved medical direction.

25. *Conditions that could raise a security concern and may be disqualifying include:*

(a) any drug abuse (see above definition);

(b) testing positive for illegal drug use;

(c) illegal drug possession, including cultivation, processing, manufacture, purchase, sale, or distribution; or possession of drug paraphernalia;

(d) diagnosis by a duly qualified medical professional (e.g., physician, clinical psychologist, or psychiatrist) of drug abuse or drug dependence;

(e) evaluation of drug abuse or drug dependence by a licensed clinical social worker who is a staff member of a recognized drug treatment program;

(f) failure to successfully complete a drug treatment program prescribed by a duly qualified medical professional;

(g) any illegal drug use after being granted a security clearance;

(h) expressed intent to continue illegal drug use, or failure to clearly and convincingly commit to discontinue drug use.

26. *Conditions that could mitigate security concerns include:*

(a) the behavior happened so long ago, was so infrequent, or happened under such circumstances that it is unlikely to recur or does not cast doubt on the individual's current reliability, trustworthiness, or good judgment;

(b) a demonstrated intent not to abuse any drugs in the future, such as:

(1) disassociation from drug-using associates and contacts;

(2) changing or avoiding the environment where drugs were used;

(3) an appropriate period of abstinence;

(4) a signed statement of intent with automatic revocation of clearance for any violation;

(c) abuse of prescription drugs was after a severe or prolonged illness during which these drugs were prescribed, and abuse has since ended;

(d) satisfactory completion of a prescribed drug treatment program, including but not limited to rehabilitation and aftercare requirements, without recurrence of abuse, and a favorable prognosis by a duly qualified medical professional.

GUIDELINE I: PSYCHOLOGICAL CONDITIONS

27. *The Concern.* Certain emotional, mental, and personality conditions can impair judgment, reliability, or trustworthiness. A formal diagnosis of a disorder is not required for there to be a concern under this guideline. A duly qualified mental health professional (e.g., clinical psychologist or psychiatrist) employed by, or acceptable to and approved by the U.S. Government, should be consulted when evaluating potentially disqualifying and mitigating information under this guideline. No negative inference concerning the standards in this Guideline may be raised solely on the basis of seeking mental health counseling.

28. *Conditions that could raise a security concern and may be disqualifying include:*

(a) behavior that casts doubt on an individual's judgment, reliability, or trustworthiness that is not covered under any other guideline, including but not limited to emotionally unstable, irresponsible, dysfunctional, violent, paranoid, or bizarre behavior;

(b) an opinion by a duly qualified mental health professional that the individual has a condition not covered under any other guideline that may impair judgment, reliability, or trustworthiness;

(c) the individual has failed to follow treatment advice related to a diagnosed emotional, mental, or personality condition, e.g., failure to take prescribed medication.

29. *Conditions that could mitigate security concerns include:*

(a) the identified condition is readily controllable with treatment, and the individual has demonstrated ongoing and consistent compliance with the treatment plan;

(b) the individual has voluntarily entered a counseling or treatment program for a condition that is amenable to treatment, and the individual is currently receiving counseling or treatment with a favorable prognosis by a duly qualified mental health professional;

(c) recent opinion by a duly qualified mental health professional employed by, or acceptable to and approved by the U.S. Government that an individual's previous condition is under control or in remission, and has a low probability of recurrence or exacerbation;

(d) the past emotional instability was a temporary condition (e.g., one caused by death, illness, or marital breakup), the situation has been resolved, and the individual no longer shows indications of emotional instability;

(e) there is no indication of a current problem.

GUIDELINE J: CRIMINAL CONDUCT

30. *The Concern.* Criminal activity creates doubt about a person's judgment, reliability, and trustworthiness. By its very nature, it calls into question a person's ability or willingness to comply with laws, rules and regulations.

31. *Conditions that could raise a security concern and may be disqualifying include:*

(a) a single serious crime or multiple lesser offenses;

(b) discharge or dismissal from the Armed Forces under dishonorable conditions;

(c) allegation or admission of criminal conduct, regardless of whether the person was formally charged, formally prosecuted or convicted;

(d) individual is currently on parole or probation;

(e) violation of parole or probation, or failure to complete a court-mandated rehabilitation program.

32. *Conditions that could mitigate security concerns include:*

(a) so much time has elapsed since the criminal behavior happened, or it happened under such unusual circumstances that it is unlikely to recur and does not cast doubt on the individual's reliability, trustworthiness, or good judgment;

(b) the person was pressured or coerced into committing the act and those pressures are no longer present in the person's life;

(c) evidence that the person did not commit the offense;

(d) there is evidence of successful rehabilitation; including but not limited to the passage of time without recurrence of criminal activity, remorse or restitution, job training or higher education, good employment record, or constructive community involvement.

GUIDELINE K: HANDLING PROTECTED INFORMATION

33. *The Concern.* Deliberate or negligent failure to comply with rules and regulations for protecting classified or other sensitive information raises doubt about an individual's trustworthiness, judgment, reliability, or willingness and ability to safeguard such information, and is a serious security concern.

34. *Conditions that could raise a security concern and may be disqualifying include:*

(a) deliberate or negligent disclosure of classified or other protected information to unauthorized persons, including but not limited to personal or business contacts, to the media, or to persons present at seminars, meetings, or conferences;

(b) collecting or storing classified or other protected information in any unauthorized location;

(c) loading, drafting, editing, modifying, storing, transmitting, or otherwise handling classified reports, data, or other information on any unapproved equipment including but not limited to any typewriter, word processor, or computer hardware, software, drive, system, gameboard, handheld, "palm" or pocket device or other adjunct equipment;

(d) inappropriate efforts to obtain or view classified or other protected information outside one's need to know;

(e) copying classified or other protected information in a manner designed to conceal or remove classification or other document control markings;

(f) viewing or downloading information from a secure system when the information is beyond the individual's need-to-know;

(g) any failure to comply with rules for the protection of classified or other sensitive information;

(h) negligence or lax security habits that persist despite counseling by management.

(i) failure to comply with rules or regulations that results in damage to the National Security, regardless of whether it was deliberate or negligent.

35. *Conditions that could mitigate security concerns include*:

(a) so much time has elapsed since the behavior, or it has happened so infrequently or under such unusual circumstances, that it is unlikely to recur and does not cast doubt on the individual's current reliability, trustworthiness, or good judgment;

(b) the individual responded favorably to counseling or remedial security training and now demonstrates a positive attitude toward the discharge of security responsibilities;

(c) the security violations were due to improper or inadequate training.

GUIDELINE L: OUTSIDE ACTIVITIES

36. *The Concern*. Involvement in certain types of outside employment or activities is of security concern if it poses a conflict of interest with an individual's security responsibilities and could create an increased risk of unauthorized disclosure of classified information.

37. *Conditions that could raise a security concern and may be disqualifying include:*

(a) any employment or service, whether compensated or volunteer, with:

(1) the government of a foreign country;

(2) any foreign national, organization, or other entity;

(3) a representative of any foreign interest;

(4) any foreign, domestic, or international organization or person engaged in analysis, discussion, or publication of material on intelligence, defense, foreign affairs, or protected technology;

(b) failure to report or fully disclose an outside activity when this is required.

38. *Conditions that could mitigate security concerns include:*

(a) evaluation of the outside employment or activity by the appropriate security or counterintelligence office indicates that it does not pose a conflict with an individual's security responsibilities or with the national security interests of the United States;

(b) the individual terminated the employment or discontinued the activity upon being notified that it was in conflict with his or her security responsibilities.

GUIDELINE M: USE OF INFORMATION TECHNOLOGY SYSTEMS

39. *The Concern.* Noncompliance with rules, procedures, guidelines or regulations pertaining to information technology systems may raise security concerns about an individual's reliability and trustworthiness, calling into question the willingness or ability to properly protect sensitive systems, networks, and information. Information Technology Systems include all related computer hardware, software, firmware, and data used for the communication, transmission, processing, manipulation, storage, or protection of information.

40. *Conditions that could raise a security concern and may be disqualifying include:*

(a) illegal or unauthorized entry into any information technology system or component thereof;

(b) illegal or unauthorized modification, destruction, manipulation or denial of access to information, software, firmware, or hardware in an information technology system;

(c) use of any information technology system to gain unauthorized access to another system or to a compartmented area within the same system;

(d) downloading, storing, or transmitting classified information on or to any unauthorized software, hardware, or information technology system;

(e) unauthorized use of a government or other information technology system;

(f) introduction, removal, or duplication of hardware, firmware, software, or media to or from any information technology system without authorization, when prohibited by rules, procedures, guidelines or regulations;

(g) negligence or lax security habits in handling information technology that persist despite counseling by management;

(h) any misuse of information technology, whether deliberate or negligent, that results in damage to the national security.

41. *Conditions that could mitigate security concerns include:*

16

(a) so much time has elapsed since the behavior happened, or it happened under such unusual circumstances, that it is unlikely to recur and does not cast doubt on the individual's reliability, trustworthiness, or good judgment;

(b) the misuse was minor and done only in the interest of organizational efficiency and effectiveness, such as letting another person use one's password or computer when no other timely alternative was readily available;

(c) the conduct was unintentional or inadvertent and was followed by a prompt, good-faith effort to correct the situation and by notification of supervisor.

ANNEX D

Appeals Procedures: Denial or Revocation of Access

1. Policy.

This annex establishes common appeals procedures for the denial or revocation of access to sensitive compartmented information (SCI) by entities of the Intelligence Community after adjudication pursuant to the provisions of DCID 6/4. This annex is promulgated pursuant to Executive Order 12333, Executive Order 12968, and the National Security Act of 1947, as amended. For the purposes of this annex, all references to DCID 6/4 include the basic document and all of its annexes. Any individual who has been considered for initial or continued access to SCI pursuant to the provisions of DCID 6/4 shall, to the extent provided below, be afforded an opportunity to appeal the denial or revocation of such access. This annex supersedes any and all other practices and procedures for the appeal of the denial or revocation of SCI access. This annex will not be construed to require the disclosure of classified information or information concerning intelligence sources and methods, nor will it be construed to afford an opportunity to appeal before the actual denial or revocation of SCI access. In addition, the provisions of DCID 6/4, or any other document or provision of law, will not be construed to create a liberty or property interest of any kind in the access of any individual to SCI.

2. Applicability.

This annex applies to all US Government civilian and military personnel, as well as any other individuals, including contractors and employees of contractors, who are considered for initial or continued access to SCI. This annex does not apply to decisions regarding employment and will not be construed to affect or impair public Law 88-290 or the authority of any entity to effect applicant or personnel actions pursuant to Public Law 88-290, Public Law 86-36, or other applicable law.

3. SCI Access Determination Authority.

Adjudications for access to SCI will be made in accordance with DCID 6/4 by a Determination Authority designated by the Senior Official of the Intelligence Community (SOIC) of each entity. Access to SCI shall be denied or revoked whenever it is determined that a person does not meet the security standards provided for in DCID 6/4. Any doubt about an individual's eligibility for access or continued access to SCI shall be resolved in favor of the national security and access will be denied or revoked.

4. Procedures.

    a.   Individuals will be:

        1.   Provided as comprehensive and detailed a written explanation of the basis for that determination as the national security interests of the United States and other applicable law permit.

        2.   Informed in this written explanation of their right to be represented by counsel or

other representative at their own expense; to request any documents, records or reports upon which a denial or revocation is based; and, to request the entire investigative file as permitted by the national security and other applicable law.

3. Provided within 30 days, upon request and to the extent the documents would be provided if requested under the Freedom of Information Act (5 U.S.C. 552) or the Privacy Act (5 U.S.C. 552a), as applicable, any documents, records and reports upon which a denial or revocation is based.

4. Provided an opportunity to reply in writing within 45 days of receipt of relevant documentation to request a review of the determination.

5. Provided written notice of and reasons for the results of the review, the identity of the deciding authority in accordance with operational requirements, and written notice of the right to appeal.

6. Provided an opportunity to appeal in writing to a high level panel, appointed by the SOIC, which shall be comprised of at least three members, two of whom shall be selected from outside the security field. Decisions of the panel shall be in writing, and final, except when the SOIC chooses to exercise the appeal authority personally, based on a recommendation from the panel, and provided to the individual.

7. Provided an opportunity to appear personally and to present relevant documents, materials and information at some point in the process before an adjudicative or other authority, other than the investigating entity, as determined by the SOIC. A written summary or recording of such appearance shall be made part of the applicant's or employee's security record., unless such appearance occurs in the presence of the appeals panel described in subsection a.(6) of this section, in which case the written decision of the panel shall be made part of the applicant's or employee's security record.

b. When a SOIC or their principal deputy personally certifies that a procedure set forth in this section cannot be made available in a particular case without damaging the national security interests of the United States by revealing classified information, the particular procedure shall not be made available. This certification shall be conclusive.

c. Nothing in this annex shall prohibit a SOIC from personally exercising the appeal authority in paragraph a.(6) above based upon recommendations from an appeals panel. In such case, the decision of the SOIC shall be final.

d. A SOIC may determine that the appeal procedures prescribed in this annex cannot be invoked in a manner that is consistent with the national security. In such cases, a SOIC may deny an individual an appeal pursuant to this annex and the authority delegated to the SOIC by the DCI under the National Security Act of 1947, as amended. The SOIC's determination in this regard shall be conclusive.

e. Nothing in this annex shall be deemed to preclude the DCI or the DDCI under the authority of the National Security Act of 1947, as amended, from taking any actions regarding an individual's SCI access. The DCI or DDCI may take any actions regarding an individual's SCI access without regard to any of the provisions of this or any other regulation or directive. The DCI or DDCI may consult with the agency head pertaining to any action to be taken regarding an individual's SCI access.

f. This annex does not create nor confer on any person or entity any right to administrative or judicial review of these procedures, their implementation, or decisions or actions rendered thereunder. It also does not create or confer any right, benefit, or privilege, whether substantive or procedural, for access to classified information. Finally, this annex does not create or confer any substantive or procedural right, benefit, or privilege enforceable by any party against the United States or any agency, department, or instrumentality of the executive branch, its officers or employees, for any other person.

ANNEX E

Standards for SCI Security Awareness Programs in the US Intelligence Community

Consistent with controls and procedures set forth in DCID 1/19, "Security Policy for Sensitive Compartmented Information," and its supplement, "DCID 1/19 Security Policy Manual," standards are hereby established for the SCI security education programs designed to enhance the security awareness of the US Government civilian and military personnel and private contractors working in the US Intelligence Community. Compliance with these standards is required for all departments/agencies within the Intelligence Community. Existing security awareness programs will be modified to conform with these standards. Departments/agencies will establish a documented program to ensure that training has been presented to all personnel.

All individuals nominated for or holding SCI access approval will be notified initially and annually thereafter of their responsibility to report to their cognizant security officers any activities or conduct such as described in Annex C that could conflict with their ability to protect classified information from unauthorized disclosure. Any outside employment, activities or conduct that could create real or apparent conflicts with their responsibility to protect classified information must be reported.

The security awareness requirements set forth herein are divided into three phases. Phase 1 concerns the initial indoctrination of individuals, which is normally administered before access to SCI. Phase 2 concerns the continuing security awareness program required to maintain an increased security awareness throughout the period of access. Phase 3 sets forth the final guidelines and instructions when access to SCI is terminated.

1. Initial Indoctrination.

As soon as practicable after being approved for access to SCI, personnel will receive an initial security indoctrination that will include:

   a. The need for and purpose of SCI, and the adverse effect on the national security that could result from unauthorized disclosure.

   b. The intelligence mission of the department/agency to include the reasons why intelligence information is sensitive.

   c. The administrative, personnel, physical, and other procedural security requirements of the department/agency and those requirements peculiar to specific duty assignments, including information on who to consult to determine if particular outside employment or activity might be of concern.

   d. Individual classification management responsibilities as set forth in appropriate directives and regulations to include classification/declassification guidelines and marking requirements.

e. The definitions and criminal penalties for espionage, including harboring or concealing persons; gathering, transmitting, or losing defense information; gathering or delivering defense information to aid foreign governments; photographing and sketching defense installations; unauthorized disclosure of classified information (Title 18, U.S.C., Sections 792 through 795, 797, and 798), the Internal Security Act of 1950 (Title 50, U.S.C., Section 783), the Intelligence Identities Protection Act of 1982 (Title 50, U.S.C., Sections 421 through 426) and, when appropriate, the Atomic Energy Act (Sections 224 through 227).

f. The administrative sanctions for violation or disregard for security procedures.

g. A review of the techniques employed by foreign intelligence organizations in attempting to obtain national security information.

h. Individual security responsibilities including:

1. The prohibition against discussing SCI in a non-secure area, over a non-secure telephone, or in any other manner that permits access by unauthorized persons.

2. The need to determine, before disseminating SCI, that the prospective recipient has the proper security access approval, that the SCI is needed in order to perform official duties, and that the recipient can properly protect the information.

3. The need to exercise security in activities as members of professional, commercial, scholarly or advocacy organizations that publish or discuss information on intelligence, defense or foreign affairs.

4. The continuing obligation to submit for review any planned articles, books, speeches or public statements that contain or purport to contain SCI or information relating to or derived from SCI, as specified by the nondisclosure agreements that are a prerequisite for access to SCI.

5. Obligation to report travel to or connections with countries with aggressive proactive intelligence capabilities, or contacts with foreign nationals under certain circumstances, or attempts (including blackmail, coercion and harassment) by unauthorized persons to obtain national security information, physical security deficiencies, and loss or possible compromise of SCI material.

6. Obligation to report to proper authorities all activities or conduct of an individual who has access to SCI which relates to guidelines described in Annex C, such as:

   a. Involvement in activities or sympathetic association with persons which/who unlawfully practice or advocate the overthrow or alteration of the United States Government by unconstitutional means.

   b. Foreign influence concerns/close personal association with foreign nationals.

   c. Foreign citizenship or foreign monetary interests.

   d. Sexual behavior that is criminal or reflects a lack of judgment or discretion.

e. Unwillingness to comply with rules and regulations or to cooperate with security processing.

f. Unexplained affluence or excessive indebtedness.

g. Alcohol abuse.

h. Illegal or improper drug use/involvement.

i. Apparent mental or emotional disorder(s).

j. Criminal conduct.

k. Noncompliance with security requirements.

l. Engagement in outside activities which could cause a conflict of interest.

m. Misuse of information technology systems.

7. Identification of the elements in the department/agency to which matters of security interest are to be referred.

2. Periodic Awareness Enhancement.

Each department/agency will establish a continuing security awareness program that will provide frequent exposure of personnel to security awareness material. Implementation of a continuing program may include live briefings, audiovisual presentations (e.g., video tapes, films, and slide/tape programs), printed material (e.g., posters, memorandums, pamphlets, fliers), or a combination thereof. It is essential that current information and materials be utilized. Programs should be designed to meet the particular needs of the department/agency.

a. The basic elements for this program will include, but are not limited to, the following:

1. The foreign intelligence threat (including the threats associated with foreign travel and foreign associations).

2. The technical threat.

3. Administrative, personnel, physical, and procedural security.

4. Individual classification management responsibility.

5. Criminal penalties and administrative sanctions.

6. Individual security responsibilities.

7. A review of other appropriate department/agency requirements.

b. Special security briefings/debriefings should supplement the existing security awareness programs in the following situations:

1. When an individual is designated as a courier.

2. When high risk situations are present, specifically:

a. When an individual travels, officially or unofficially, to or through countries with aggressive/proactive intelligence capabilities or with connection(s) to terrorism or criminal activity, or:

b. When an individual has, or anticipates contact with a representative(s) of the countries identified above.

3. When any other situation arises for which the SOIC or designee determines that an increased level of protection is necessary.

3. Debriefing.

When a department/agency has determined that access to SCI is no longer required, final instructions and guidelines will be provided to the individual. At a minimum these shall include:

a. A requirement that the individual read appropriate sections of Titles 18 and 50, U.S.C., and that the intent and criminal sanctions of these laws relative to espionage and unauthorized disclosure be clarified.

b. The continuing obligation, under the prepublication and other provisions of the nondisclosure agreement for SCI, never to divulge; publish; or reveal by writing, word, conduct, or otherwise, to any unauthorized persons any SCI, without the written consent of appropriate department/agency officials.

c. An acknowledgment that the individual will report without delay to the Federal Bureau of Investigation, or the department/agency, any attempt by an unauthorized person to solicit national security information.

d. A declaration that the individual no longer possesses any documents or material containing SCI.

e. A reminder of the risks associated with foreign travel and foreign association.

ANNEX F

Reciprocity of SCI Eligibility Determinations

1. Reciprocity Policy.

a. Within the Intelligence Community, subject to the conditions set forth below, a favorable DCID 6/4 eligibility determination for access to SCI made by one adjudicative authority under SOIC cognizance is a favorable determination for all SOICs. Reciprocity of eligibility determinations does not in itself constitute reciprocity of need-to-know determinations. Need-to-know determinations are always distinct and separate decisions.

b. Reciprocity requires adjudication by trained government adjudicators under SOIC cognizance and a system for monitoring continuing security eligibility. Eligibility decisions, including the presence of exceptions, must be a matter of record accessible to the Intelligence Community's access granting authorities.

c. DCID 6/4 eligibility determinations are mutually acceptable and will not be readjudicated if:

   1. They are made without exception, and

   2. No substantial issue information exists since the most recent adjudication, and

   3. The appropriate type of polygraph examination, if one is required, has been satisfactorily completed.

d. Agencies may accept or reject DCID 6/4 eligibility determinations where exceptions exist based upon their own assessment of risk. Any agency rejecting another's determination of eligibility where exceptions exist will notify, to extent it is able to do so, all adjudicative authorities having an eligibility interest in the person of it decision. Those authorities, in turn, *may* reassess the appropriateness of continuing to hold the person eligible with an exception.

e. Where an agency or organization has additional but not duplicative requirements, the actual granting of access is contingent upon satisfying those requirements. Failure to meet an additional but not duplicative requirement may not necessarily adversely affect a person's continued eligibility for reciprocal access with other organizations and agencies. However, the agency that made the original eligibility determinations may use new information obtained by another organization to readjudicate the person's continued eligibility subject to restrictions placed on use of the information by the organization that obtained it.

f. A person determined ineligible for SCI access will remain ineligible for a minimum of one year. However, SOICs or their designees may waive this requirement in individual.

g. This annex does not apply to suitability decisions for employment.

2. Definitions.

a. *Exception:* An adjudicative decision to grant or continue access eligibility despite a failure to meet adjudicative or investigative standards. Regarding SCI access eligibility, only the DCI or, as appropriate, the concerned Senior Official of the Intelligence Community (SOIC) or designee will make such decisions. An exception precludes reciprocity without review of the case by the gaining organization or program. There are three types:

1. *Condition:* Access eligibility granted or continued with the provision that one or more additional measures will be required. Such measures include additional security monitoring, restrictions on access, and restrictions on the individual's handling of classified information. Submission of periodic financial statements, admonishment regarding use of drugs or excessive use of alcohol, and satisfactory progress in a government-approved counseling program are examples of conditions.

2. *Deviation:* Access eligibility granted or continued despite either a significant gap in coverage or scope in the investigation or an out-of-date investigation. "significant gap" for this purpose means either complete lack of coverage for a period of six months or more within the most recent five years investigated or lack of an FBI name check or technical check or the lack of one or more relevant investigative scope components (e.g., employment checks or a subject interview for an SSBI, financial review for any investigation) in its entirety.

3. *Waiver.* Access eligibility granted or continued despite the presence of substantial issue information that would normally preclude access. The DCI, SOIC, or SOIC's designee approve waivers pursuant to their authorities outlined in DCID 6/4, paragraphs 6a and b, only when the benefit of access clearly outweighs any security concern raised by the shortcoming. A waiver may require special limitations on access, additional security monitoring and restrictions on the person's handling of classified information beyond normal need-to-know. Paragraph 6 of DCID 6/4 governs the granting of waivers insofar as they pertain to SCI access eligibility. In the Intelligence Community, waivers may be contemplated when the person under consideration for SCI access is not a United States citizen, when any member of that person's immediate family is not a US citizen, or when any member of the immediate family or other person with whom there is a bond of affection or obligation is subject to duress.

b. *Issue information.* Any information that could adversely affect a person's eligibility for access to classified information. There are two types:

1. *Minor issue information:* Information that meets a threshold of concern set out in "Adjudicative Guidelines for Determining Eligibility for Access to Classified Information" (see Annex C to DCID 6/4), but for which adjudication determines that adequate mitigation's, as provided for by the Guidelines, exists. Minor issue information does *not* provide the basis for a waiver or condition.

2. *Substantial issue information:* Any information, or aggregate of information,

that raises a significant question about the prudence of granting access eligibility. Substantial issue information constitutes the basis for granting access eligibility with waiver or condition, or for denying or revoking access eligibility. Granting access eligibility when substantial issue information exists is predicated upon meeting the requirements of paragraphs 12a and b of DCID 6/4 for tailored security programs whose purpose is to resolve issues.

c. *Need to Know:* A determinations made by an authorized holder of classified information that a prospective recipient requires access to specific classified information in order to perform or assist in a lawful and authorized governmental function.

d. *Reciprocity:* Acceptance by one SOIC of an SCI access eligibility determination made by another. It applies both to granting access when another SOIC has approved and denying access when another SOIC has denied or revoked. Reciprocity does not include agency determinations of employment suitability. Nothing precludes SOICs or their designees from exercising authority to grant or to deny access for reasons of operational necessity regardless of another SOIC's decision.

3. The effect of the Polygraph on Reciprocity.

The Intelligence Community uses the polygraph in defined circumstances to provide additional information to the adjudicative process. Reciprocity of an SCI eligibility determination when a polygraph requirement exists is conditional upon satisfactory completion of that requirement.

4. Review of access Determinations.

All denial or revocations of access eligibility are subject to the review proceedings outlined in Annex D, above.

Footnotes:

1 DCID 1/14 was renumbered 6/4 by the Director of Central Intelligence (DCI) and the Deputy Director of Central Intelligence for Community Management on 13 Oct 99, to more closely align the DCID with the new category structure as defined in DCID 1/1. This action was accomplished in conjunction with the DCI approving the newly created Annex F, "Reciprocity of SCI Eligibility Determinations".

2 The content of this Annex is taken verbatim from the Presidentially approved Investigative Standards and Temporary Eligibility Standards and should be read in the context of access eligibility to SCI, although the actual wording addresses a broader application to clearance actions.

3 The content of this Annex is taken verbatim from the Presidentially approved Adjudicative Guidelines and should be read in the context of access eligibility to SCI, although the actual

wording addresses a broader application to clearance actions.

4 The adjudicator should also consider guidelines pertaining to criminal conduct (Guideline J) and emotional, mental, and personality disorders (Guideline I) in determining how to resolve the security concerns raised by sexual behavior.

5 Annex F was signed by the DCI on 13 Oct 99. At that time, the number of DCID 1/14 was changed to 6/4 to correspond to an appropriate section in DCID 1/1

www.ingramcontent.com/pod-product-compliance
Lightning Source LLC
Chambersburg PA
CBHW080555290526
45790CB00006B/2655